the GOLFER'S BOOK of WIT & WISDOM

THE COMPLETE COLLECTION OF GOLF JOKES, ONE-LINERS AND WITTY SAYINGS

Hatherleigh Press is committed to preserving
and protecting the natural resources of the earth.
Environmentally responsible and sustainable practices are
embraced within the company's mission statement.

Visit us at www.hatherleighpress.com and register online
for free offers, discounts, special events, and more.

The Golfer's Book of Wit & Wisdom

Library of Congress Cataloging-in-Publication Data is available.
ISBN: 978-1-57826-840-5

Printed in the United States
10 9 8 7 6 5 4 3 2 1

Contents

Introduction   *v*

The Great Game of Golf   1

Golf (According to Non-Golfers)   15

Understanding Golfers   36

Golf Etiquette   51

Putters, Drivers & Patience   75

On Caddies   87

Putts, Puns & Golf Jokes   93

Hole-In-One   119

As in Golf, So in Life   127

Conclusion   *137*

Introduction

The importance of golf in the history of sportsmanship cannot be overstated. From professional play to the casual match, golfing has cultivated a large community of people, all striving for one thing: the perfect ace. Every first tee is the beginning of 18 rounds that can bring to fruition new business deals, new friendships, and priceless time spent outdoors. Golfing is good for the mind, body, and spirit, and provides a wealth of benefits that other sports only dream of.

This book aims to convey the feeling of a great match through the words of golfing's best and brightest, with a good laugh peppered throughout. So take a break, read a few of these quotes, and share some wit and wisdom the next time you hit the field.

The Great Game of Golf

Golf is a game of misses. Whoever misses best is going to win.

—BEN HOGAN

Golf is an awkward set of bodily contortions designed to produce a graceful result.

—TOMMY ARMOUR

Golf is a game where you can always find someone to beat and someone who will beat you.

—SANDY PARR

Golf—a game in which you claim the privileges of age, and retain the playthings of childhood.

—SAMUEL JOHNSON

Golf is a game in which a ball one and a half inches in diameter is placed on a ball 8,000 miles in diameter. The object is to hit the small ball but not the larger.

—JOHN CUNNINGHAM

Golf is a game of precision, not strength.

—JACK NICKLAUS

Golf is a spiritual game. It's like Zen. You have to let your mind take over.

—AMY STRUM ALCOTT

Golf is a game that is played on a five inch course—the distance between your ears.

—ANONYMOUS

Golf is the best game in the world at which to be bad...It is the bad player who gets the most strokes.

—A.A. MILNE

Golf is just a game of marbles for boys who don't want to bend down.

—YOUP VAN 'T HEK

Golf is the only sport where the ball doesn't move until you hit it.

—TED WILLIAMS

Golf is a lot like taxes: you drive hard to get to green and then wind up in the hole.

—H. GORDON HAVENS

Golf is in the interest of good health and good manners. It promotes self-restraint and affords a chance to play the man and act the gentleman.

—WILLIAM HOWARD TAFT

There are three things that are as unfathomable as they are fascinating to the masculine mind: metaphysics, the feminine heart and golf.

—ARNOLD HAULTAIN

Golf has probably kept more people sane than psychiatrists have.

—HARVEY PENICK

There's no such thing as bad weather for a dedicated golfer.

—SANDY PARR

Golf is evolving, every day, every shot.

—TIGER WOODS

Golf is a game of ego, but it is also a game of integrity, the most important thing is you do what is right when no one is looking.

—TOM WATSON

Golf may be played on a Sunday: not being a game within the view of the law, but being a form of moral effort.

—STEPHEN B. LEACOCK

If there is any larceny in a man, golf will bring it out.

—PAUL GALLICO

Golf is harder than baseball. In golf, you have to play your foul balls.

—BERYL DERANGED

The difference between golf and government is that in golf you can't improve your lie.

—GEORGE DEUKMEJIAN

Tennis is a sport, golf is a game.

—PAUL HAARHUIS

Golf is like a love affair: if you don't take it seriously, it's no fun; if you do take it seriously, it breaks your heart.

—ARNOLD DALY

Eighteen holes of golf will teach you more about your foe than eighteen years of dealing with him across a desk.

—GRANTLAND RICE

Golf is happiness.

—MOE NORMAN

If a woman can walk, she can play golf.

—LOUISE SUGGS

I adore the game of golf. I won't ever retire. I'll play until I die. Then I want them to roll me into a bunker, cover me with sand and make sure nobody's ball lands there for a while.

—PETER DARBO

Golf is deceptively simple and endlessly complicated.

—BERYL DERANGED

Never jog on a golf course. You could run into a string of double bogeys.

—CHARLES SCHULZ

If you break 100, watch your golf. If you break 80, watch your business.

—JOEY ADAMS

Pressure is playing for $50 a hole with only $5 in your pocket.

—LEE TREVINO

Don't praise your own good shots. Leave that function to your partner who, if a good sport, will not be slow in performing it.

—HARRY VARDON

A golf course is nothing but a poolroom moved outdoors.

—LEO MCCAREY

Golf is the Great Mystery.

—P.G. WODEHOUSE

Golf is a puzzle without an answer. I've played the game for 50 years and I still haven't the slightest idea of how to play.

—GARY PLAYER

Don't underestimate how expensive a hobby golf can be.

—SANDY PARR

I find it more satisfying to be a bad player at golf. The worse you play, the better you remember the occasional good shot.

—NUBAR GULBENKIAN

You must work very hard to become a natural golfer.

—GARY PLAYER

Golf will grow so long as it's fun.

—TOM WATSON

GOLF

(According to Non-Golfers)

Golf is just an expensive way of walking.

—MICHAEL PARKINSON

Golf is a lot of walking, broken up by disappointment and bad arithmetic.

—PETER DARBO

Golf is a game in which one endeavors to control a ball with implements ill adapted for the purpose.

—WOODROW WILSON

Golf is not a sport. Golf is men in ugly pants, walking.

—ROSIE O'DONNELL

Golf—the unthinkable in pursuit of the unsinkable.

—DOUGLAS WATKINSON

Golf—pool played on a larger table.

—SANDY PARR

Golf is an expensive way of playing marbles.

—G.K. CHESTERTON

Golf is the only game where the worst player gets the best of it. He obtains more out of it as regards both exercise and enjoyment, for the good player gets worried over the slightest mistake, whereas the poor player makes too many mistakes to worry over them.

—DAVID LLOYD GEORGE

Golf is the only game, outside of solitaire, where you play alone. What you do with your ball hasn't got anything to do with what the other fellow does with his. It's solitaire, only quieter.

—WILL ROGERS

Golf—a game to be played between cricket and death.

—COLIN INGLEBY-MCKENZIE

Golf is a good walk spoiled.

—MARK TWAIN

Golf is the loneliest of all games, not excluding postal chess.

—PETER DOBEREINER

Golf—one of the few games where the better you play, the less you see of the ball.

—SANDY PARR

Golf is a fascinating game. It has taken me nearly forty years to discover that I can't play it.

—TED RAY

Golf is a game that was invented to punish those who retire early.

—PETER DARBO

Golf is the only game in which you fail to win 99 per cent of the time.

—CHRIS PLUMRIDGE

One of the advantages bowling has over golf is that you seldom lose a bowling ball.

—DON CARTER

Golf is the cruelest game, because eventually it will drag you out in front of the whole school, take your lunch money and slap you around.

—RICK REILLY

Golf is a game that needlessly prolongs the lives of some of our most useless citizens.

—BOB HOPE

Golf—the game that makes men forget they are married.

—CY DEBOER

Golf is a game whose aim is to hit a very small ball into an even smaller hole, with weapons singularly ill-designed for the purpose.

—WINSTON CHURCHILL

Golf is the only game in the world in which a precise knowledge of the rules can earn you a reputation for bad sportsmanship.

—PATRICK CAMPBELL

Golf is a game with the soul of a 1956 Rotarian.

—BILL MANDEL

Golf is the most useless outdoor game ever devised to waste the time and try the spirit of man.

—WESTBROOK PEGLER

Golf is a dull game. The players are dull robots carrying sticks. They don't even spit or scratch their privates like other athletes.

—LEWIS GRIZZARD

Golf is a game in which the ball lies poorly and the players well.

—ART ROSENBAUM

Golf is a game designed by a sadist for millions of masochists.

—BRIAN BARNES

Golf can best be defined as an endless series of tragedies obscured by the occasional miracle, followed by a good bottle of beer.

—BILL SADGARDEN

Golf is an ideal diversion but a ruinous disease.

—B.C. FORBES

Golf is something you did with your hands while you talked. Unless you smoked—then you never had to leave the clubhouse.

—ERMA BOMBECK

Golf is not so much a sport as an insult to lawns.

—DAVE BARRY

Golf is a great weekend sport. It makes going back to work on Monday seem almost a relief.

—PETER DARBO

Golf—an excuse for carrying unconcealed weapons and a Scotch breath.

—GIDEON WURDZ

It is now not generally believed that golf originated in Scotland. No Scotsman would invent a game in which it was possible to lose a ball.

—DES MACHALE

Golf is the only sport where the most feared opponent is you.

—DAVID POTTER

The game of golf fulfils the axioms laid down for a perfect exercise—a walk with an object.

—JAMES CANTLIE

Golf is a typical capitalist lunacy of upper-class Edwardian England.

—GEORGE BERNARD SHAW

Golf: a plague invented by the Calvinistic Scots as a punishment for man's sins.

—JAMES RESTON

Golf—the most popular method of beating round the bush.

—LEOPOLD FECHTNER

If God had intended a round of golf to take more than three hours, He would not have invented Sunday lunch.

—JIMMY HILL

Golf is a day spent in a round of strenuous idleness.

—WILLIAM WORDSWORTH

Golf is the cocaine of the correct, the rock-and-roll of the elderly.

—NIALL TOIBIN

Talking about golf is always boring.

—DAVE BARRY

I was summoned to appear before the golf club committee for playing off the ladies' tee. I explained I was playing my third shot.

—BING CROSBY

Golf is good for the soul. You get so mad at yourself you forget to hate your enemies.

—WILL ROGERS

Another name for golf is 'disappointment'.

—CHRIS PLUMRIDGE

The one reward that golf has given me, and I shall always be thankful for it, is introducing me to some of the world's most picturesque, tireless and bald-faced liars.

—RING LARDNER

Nothing counts in golf like your opponent.

—JOEY ADAMS

Of all the games man has devised, supposedly for his enjoyment, golf is in a class by itself in the anguish it inflicts.

—H.W. WIND

Golf...is the infallible test. The man who can go into a patch of rough alone, with the knowledge that only God is watching him, and play his ball where it lies, is the man who will serve you faithfully and well.

—P.G. WODEHOUSE

Golf appeals to the idiot in us and the child. Just how childlike golf players become is proven by their frequent inability to count past five.

—JOHN UPDIKE

I guess there is nothing that will get your mind off everything like golf. I have never been depressed enough to take up the game, but they say you get so sore at yourself you forget to hate your enemies.

—WILL ROGERS

Golf—cow pasture pool.

—O.K. BOVARD

Golf…combines two favorite American pastimes: taking long walks and hitting things with a stick. Try to tailor your golfing behavior to the low-key, low-pressure spirit of these antecedents. Calm the nerves of fellow players by talking cheerfully to them while they tee off or attempt to one-putt. Help the greenkeeper do his job by making sure that grass roots are well-aerated with divots. Give the caddy a chance to catch up on his aerobic exercises trotting alongside the golf cart with your bag on his shoulder. And don't hit things you aren't supposed to. An important aspect of golf is knowing what to hit.

—P.J. O'ROURKE

Golf is not a sport; it's a career move.

—MIKE BULLEN

All games are silly, but golf, if you look at it dispassionately, goes to extremes.

—PETER ALLISS

Golf has drawbacks. It is possible, by too much of it, to destroy the mind... Excessive golfing dwarfs the intellect. Nor is this to be wondered at when we consider the more fatuously vacant the mind is, the better for play. It has been observed that absolute idiots play the steadiest.

—WALTER SIMPSON

His friends call it madness, but he calls it golf.

—LEOPOLD FECHTNER

A triple bogey is three strokes more than par, four strokes more than par is a quadruple bogey, five more than par is a quintuple, six is a sextuple, seven is a throwuple, eight is a blowuple, and nine is an ohshutuple.

—HENRY BEARD

All I've got against golf is that it takes you so far from the clubhouse.

—ERIC LINKLATER

I play golf even though I hate it. I'm not done with a game yet. I hate those windmills.

—MARK GUIDO

The game of golf would lose a great deal if croquet mallets and billiard cues were allowed on the putting green.

—ERNEST HEMINGWAY

Love and putting are mysteries for the philosopher to solve. Both subjects are beyond golfers.

—TOMMY ARMOUR

I don't want to play golf. When I hit a ball, I want someone else to go chase it.

—ROGERS HORNSBY

Golf does not run well on vengeance.
In golf, the harder you try, the worse you do.

—RICK REILLY

Golfing excellence goes hand in hand with alcohol, as many an open mind and amateur champion has shown.

—HENRY LONGHURST

Understanding Golfers

Golf is played by twenty million mature American men whose wives think they are out having fun.

—JIM BISHOP

Golfer: a guy who has the advantage over a fisherman—he doesn't have to bring home anything when he brags he had a great day.

—GEECHY GUY

The ardent golfer would play Mount Everest if somebody would put a flagstick on top.

—PETE DYE

Real golfers tape the Masters so they can go play themselves.

—GEORGE ROOPE

Real golfers don't cry when they line up their fourth putt.

—KAREN HURWITZ

A really good golfer is one who always knows what your score is.

—O.A. BATTISTA

A good golfer has the determination to win and the patience to wait for the breaks.

—GARY PLAYER

A golfer needs a loving wife to whom he can describe the day's play through the long evening.

—P.G. WODEHOUSE

Golfers hate cake because they might get a slice.

—TONY THOENNES

Let me get this straight: The less I hit the ball, the better I am doing...
Then why do it at all?

—JOHNNY HART

If the golfer's object was merely to sink the ball in the hole, he could walk around the course with a bag of golf balls and drop each one in.

—ARNOLD LUNN

A coarse golfer is one who normally goes from tee to green without touching the fairway.

—MICHAEL GREEN

An old timer is one who remembers when he hit a golf ball it went as far as he expected it to.

—O.A. BATTISTA

One way to solve the problem of golfers' slow play is to knock the ball into them. There will be a short delay while you have a hell of a fight, but from then on they'll move faster.

—HORACE HUTCHINSON

Real golfers go to work to relax.

—GEORGE DILLON

The true coarse golfer takes a divot when he putts.

—MILTON BERLE

Give me a man with big hands, big feet and no brains and I will make a golfer out of him.

—WALTER C. HAGEN

A golfer who can chip and putt is a match for anybody. A golfer who cannot is a match for nobody.

—SANDY PARR

It is not mere technical skill that makes a man a golfer, it is the golfing soul.

—P.G. WODEHOUSE

They say "practice" makes perfect. Of course, it doesn't; for the vast majority of golfers it merely consolidates imperfection.

—HENRY LONGHURST

If you come in second, you're just the first loser!

—TIGER WOODS

Real golfers, no matter what the provocation, never strike a caddie with the driver. The sand wedge is far more effective.

—HUXTABLE PIPPEY

The person I fear most in the last two rounds
is myself.

—TOM WATSON

The only thing a golfer needs is more daylight.

—BEN HOGAN

A natural golfer can afford to believe that anyone
with the coordination to walk and chew gum
at the same time should be able to sink a putt
under stress.

—STEVE ALLEN

Statisticians estimate that crime among good golfers is lower than in any class of the community except possibly bishops.

—P.G. WODEHOUSE

Golfers don't fist fight. They cuss a bit. But they wouldn't punch anything or anybody. They might hurt their hands and have to change their grip.

—DAN JENKINS

A great golf course both frees and challenges a golfer's mind.

—TOM WATSON

A man who can putt is a match for anyone.

—WILLIE PARK

Golfers are among the most deluded of sports-men and women, clinging to the belief that no matter how badly they perform, tomorrow it will be better.

—CHRIS PLUMRIDGE

For a golfer, to be "in form" means: the moment that the unconscious easily performs what the conscious is hoping for.

—FREEK DE JONGE

Nothing improves a golfer's disposition like finding a better ball than he went looking for.

—O.A. BATTISTA

Golf Etiquette

All is fair in love and golf.

—AMERICAN PROVERB

There is only one main rule in golf. Hit the ball until it gets into the hole.

—MILES KINGTON

The simple thing about golf is that it is relatively easy to spell.

—CHRIS PLUMRIDGE

Golf has more rules than any other game, because golf has more cheaters than any other game.

—BRUCE LANSKY

Golfers who know the rules backwards are to be avoided.

—CHRIS PLUMRIDGE

Always tell the truth. You may make a hole in one when you're alone on the golf course someday.

—FRANKLIN P. JONES

Always play a game with somebody, never against them. Always win a game, never beat an opponent.

—ANDREW BAILEY

Always fade the ball; you can't talk to a hook.

—DAVE MARR

Standing still is one of the most important parts of the game.

—PETER COOK

If you're serious about improving your play, be brutally honest with yourself.

—GREG NORMAN

Don't play too much golf. Two rounds a day are plenty.

—HARRY VARDON

Most people play a fair game of golf—if you watch them.

—JOEY ADAMS

The most successful way to play golf is the easiest way.

—HARRY VARDON

Placing the ball in the right position for the next shot is eighty percent of winning golf.

—BEN HOGAN

The easiest shot in golf is the fourth putt.

—RING LARDNER

Take less time to read the scorecard and more time to read the hole.

—CHI CHI RODRIGUEZ

There is no similarity between golf and putting; they are two different games; one played in the air, and the other on the ground.

—BEN HOGAN

The big trick in putting is not method, the secret of putting is domination of the nerves.

—HENRY COTTON

Remember that you hit the ball further by hitting it better, not harder.

—SANDY PARR

Tee the ball high. Because years of experience have shown me that air offers less resistance to dirt.

—JACK NICKLAUS

Feel is the most perplexing part of golf, and probably the most important.

—ARNOLD PALMER

Nothing handicaps you so much in golf as honesty.

—PETER DARBO

Truth is something you leave in the locker room with your street shoes when you play golf.

—GENE PERRET

To play well you must feel tranquil and at peace. I have never been troubled by nerves in golf because I felt I had nothing to lose and everything to gain.

—HARRY VARDON

If you can't win fairly, you don't deserve to win.

—STEELE BISHOP

Drive for show. But putt for dough.

—BOBBY LOCKE

Achievements on the golf course are not what matters; decency and honesty are what matters.

—TIGER WOODS

Golf is not just to win. It is to play like a gentleman, and win.

—PHIL MICKELSON

Nobody asked how you looked, just what you shot.

—SAM SNEAD

If you ever feel sorry for somebody at a golf course, you better go home. If you don't kill them, they'll kill you.

—SEVE BALLESTEROS

If you wish to hide your character, do not play golf.

—PERCEY BOOMER

The secret of missing a tree is to aim straight at it.

—MICHAEL GREEN

Golf is like solitaire. When you cheat, you only cheat yourself.

—TONY LEMA

Golf is a matter of confidence. If you think you cannot do it, there is no chance you will.

—PETER DARBO

Golfers have analyzed the game in order to find "the secret." There is no secret.

—HENRY COTTON

Whenever you think you hit the green you wouldn't.

—TEODORO CORREA

Make the hard ones look easy and the easy ones look hard.

—WALTER HAGEN

Hit the ball up to the hole. You meet a better class of person there.

—BEN HOGAN

You build a golf game like you build a wall, one brick at a time.

—TONY LEMA

The newer the golf ball the more likely you are to lose it.

—CHRIS PLUMRIDGE

Success in golf depends less on strength of body than upon strength of mind and character.

—ARNOLD PALMER

The most important distance in golf is the distance between the ears.

—SANDY PARR

Every shot counts. The three-foot putt is just as important as the 300-yard drive.

—HENRY COTTON

Thinking instead of acting is the number one disease in golf.

—SAM SNEAD

Take it easy and lazily, because the golf ball isn't going to run away from you while you're swinging.

—SAM SNEAD

Look like a woman, but play like a man.

—JAN STEPHENSON

A couple of hours of practice is worth ten sloppy rounds.

—BABE DIDRIKSON ZAHARIAS

A golf ball can stop in the fairway, rough, woods, bunker or lake. With five equally like options, very few balls choose the fairway.

—JIM BISHOP

Anybody who can keep his eye on the ball is bound to be a success, especially if he likes golf.

—O.A. BATTISTA

You gotta learn how to play golf in the rain.

—JOSEPH COOK

In golf, the ball always lies poorly; and the player well.

—PETER DARBO

A golf ball will always travel furthest when hit in the wrong direction.

—HENRY BEARD

By the time you get to your ball, if you don't know what to do with it, try another sport.

—JULIUS BOROS

That little white ball won't move 'til you hit it, and there's nothing you can do after it's gone.

—BABE DIDRIKSON ZAHARIAS

Putting allows the touchy golfer two to four opportunities to blow a gasket in the short space of two to forty feet.

—TOMMY BOLT

The average golfer doesn't play golf, he attacks it.

—JACK BURKE

When you're prepared, you're more confident. When you have a strategy, you're more comfortable.

—FRED COUPLES

You can hit a 200 acre fairway 10 per cent of the time and a two-inch branch 90 per cent of the time.

—HENRY BEARD

Practice puts brains in your muscles.

—SAM SNEAD

If there is a thunderstorm on a golf course, walk down the middle of the fairway holding a one-iron over your head. Even God can't hit a one-iron.

—LEE TREVINO

The only sure rule in golf is—he who has the fastest cart never has to play the bad lie.

—MICKEY MANTLE

Second guesses in putting are fatal.

—BOBBY LOCKE

Play every shot so that the next one will be the easiest that you can give yourself.

—BILLY CASPER

There are three things a man must do alone—testify, die and putt.

—BENNETT CERF

Golf, like measles, should be caught young, for, if postponed to riper years, the results may be serious.

—P.G. WODEHOUSE

Putts should be conceded only in the following circumstances:

(i)   When your opponent is two inches from the pin and three down.

(ii) Your opponent is nine feet from the hole and is your boss.

(iii) Immediately after you have holed out in one.

—TOM SCOTT

If you call on God to improve the results of a shot while it is still in motion, you are using 'an outside agency' and subject to appropriate penalties under the rules of golf.

—HENRY LONGHURST

I have a tip that can take five strokes off anyone's golf game.
It's called an eraser.

—ARNOLD PALMER

Safety is needed in order to play golf in a vault.

—JOSEPH LEFF

Think ahead. Golf is a next-shot game.

—BILLY CASPER

Putters, Drivers & Patience

You play golf on your own with a club.

—FREEK DE JONGE

Never break your putter and your driver in the same round or you're dead.

—TOMMY BOLT

Golf club: a stick with a head on one end and a fool at the other.

—DAMIEN MULDOON

Golf ball: a sphere made of rubber bands wound up about half as tensely as the man trying to hit it.

—PETER DARBO

A tap-in is a putt that is short enough to be missed one-handed.

—HENRY BEARD

I'm using a new putter because the old one didn't float too well.

—CRAIG STADLER

If you are going to throw a club, it is important to throw it ahead of you, down the fairway, so you don't have to waste energy going back to pick it up.

—TOMMY BOLT

Don't buy a putter until you've had a chance to throw it.

—PETER DARBO

You can take a man's wife, you can even take his wallet. But never on any account take a man's putter.

—ARCHIE COMPSTON

When you are putting well, you are a good putter; when your opponent is putting well, he has a good putter.

—JOHN D. SHERIDAN

Corollary: clubs don't float.

—BERYL DERANGED

Confidence builds with successive putts. The putter, then, is a club designed to hit the ball partway to the hole.

—RING LARDNER

If you can't wiggle your toes around in your golf shoes, they are either a size too small or you are standing too far away from the ball.

—SANDY PARR

The other day I broke 70. That's a lot of clubs.

—HENNY YOUNGMAN

The trouble that most of us find with the modern matched sets of clubs is that they don't really seem to know any more about the game than the old ones did.

—ROBERT BROWNING

Golf cart: a vehicle with a fore cylinder engine.

—DARYL STOUT

A perfectly straight shot with a big club is a fluke.

—JACK NICKLAUS

My car absolutely will not run unless my golf clubs are in the trunk.

—BRUCE BERLET

Happiness is a long walk with a putter.

—GREG NORMAN

They have some new equipment in golf now that favors seniors. Ike that long putter you put right under your chin. You can putt and take a nap at the same time.

—GENE PERRET

It takes a lot of courage to want to be buried with your golf clubs. Imagine carrying a bag of golf clubs and trying to convince St. Peter that you never told a lie.

—BERYL DERANGED

If you think it's difficult to meet new people, try picking up the wrong golf ball.

—JACK LEMMON

A golf ball is no substitute for a boiled egg.

—KEES VAN KOOTEN

Try to think where you want to put the ball not where you don't want it to go.

—BILLY CASPER

All it takes to upset a serious golfer is one high ball.

—O.A. BATTISTA

By the time a man can afford to lose a golf ball, he can't hit it that far.

—LEWIS GRIZZARD

Whenever you think you might finish a 9-holes play with one ball, it won't.

—BERYL DERANGED

Don't be in such a hurry. That little white ball isn't going to run away from you.

—PATTY BERG

A ball you can see in the rough from 50 yards away is not yours.

—PETER DARBO

If there is a ball in the fringe and a ball in the bunker, your ball is in the bunker. If both balls are in the bunker, yours is in the footprint.

—VICKY SATTER

The ultimate judge of your swing is the flight of the ball.

—BEN HOGAN

I've never lost a golf ball—I've never hit one far enough to lose one.

—BERYL DERANGED

Do you know what happens when you slice a
golf ball in half?
Someone gets mad at you. I found this out the
hard way.

—JACK HANDEY

And the wind shall say: 'Here were decent
godless people:
Their only monument the asphalt road
And a thousand lost golf balls.'

—T.S. ELIOT

On Caddies

Caddie: someone who accompanies the golfer and didn't see the ball either.

—JOE FRANCIS

The only useful putting advice I ever got from my caddy was to keep the ball low.

—CHI CHI RODRIGUEZ

Real golfers, whatever the provocation, never strike the caddy with a driver. A sand wedge is far more effective.

—BRIAN BARNES

If your caddie says to you on the tee, "Hit it down the left side with a little draw", ignore him. All you do on the tee is try not to hit the caddie.

—JIM MURRAY

I never kick my ball in the rough or improve my lie in a sand trap. For that, I have a caddy.

—BOB HOPE

The only time I talk on a golf course is to my caddie. And then only to complain when he gives me the wrong club.

—SEVE BALLESTEROS

I told the caddie I wanted a sand wedge and he brought me a ham on rye.

—CHI CHI RODRIGUEZ

On the golf course nobody really cares what happens to you except you and your caddy. And if he's bet against you, he doesn't care either.

—LEE TREVINO

If it weren't for golf, I'd probably be a caddie today.

—GEORGE ARCHER

Isn't it amazing the way carts have taken the place of caddies on the golf course? Let's face it—they have three big advantages: They don't cost; they don't criticize; and they don't count.

—ROBERT ORBEN

Caddie: a small boy, employed at a liberal stipend, to lose balls for others and find them for himself.

—HAL ROACH

After shooting over 200 I asked my partner
what I should give the caddie. He replied, "Your
golf clubs".

—JACKIE GLEASON

While tearing off
A game of golf
I may make a play for the caddy.
But when I do
I don't follow through
'Cause my heart belongs to Daddy.

—COLE PORTER

Putts, Puns & Golf Jokes

No new golf joke has been invented for 40 years.

—MICHAEL GREEN

If you drink, don't drive. Don't even putt.

—DEAN MARTIN

Golf: a hole in the market.

—HUUB MARTRON

It is now known that Darwin was a golfer—he set out in search of the missing links.

—SAM GROSS

Golf is a sport in which a small white ball is chased by men who are too old to chase anything else.

—E.C. MCKENZIE

Golf is the most fun you can have without taking your clothes off.

—CHI CHI RODRIGUEZ

Golf: a market in a hole.

—DAVID POTTER

Playing golf with the President is handy. If you hit a ball into the rough and it drops near a tree, the tree becomes a Secret Service man and moves away.

—BOB HOPE

What do I think of Tiger Woods? I don't know; I've never played there.

—SANDY LYLE

Seve Ballesteros hits the ball further than I go on my holidays.

—LEE TREVINO

One of the best ways to help a man get out of the woods is to find the golf ball he's looking for.

—O.A. BATTISTA

They call it golf because all the other good four-letter words were already taken.

—LEWIS GRIZZARD

If you want a good golf swing adjust the nut at the other end of the club!

—GRANT MCKAY

Columbus went around the world in 1492. That isn't a lot of strokes when you consider the course.

—LEE TREVINO

A dog makes a good golfing companion, especially if you can teach it to find lost balls.

—SANDY PARR

It's good sportsmanship not to pick up lost balls while they are still rolling.

—MARK TWAIN

You can tell a boss and the employee. The employee is the one who makes a hole-in-one and says, "Oops!"

—BOB MONKHOUSE

I'm a scratch golfer. I write down all my good scores and scratch out all my bad ones.

—CHARLES SCHULZ

Doctors who golf have one advantage over the rest: nobody can read their scorecards.

—NOEL V. GINNITY

Give me my golf clubs, fresh air and a beautiful girl, and you can keep my golf clubs and the fresh air.

—JACK BENNY

Where I play golf, the course has 150 holes. The greenskeeper has a wooden leg.

—BERYL DERANGED

When I won the golf challenge in South Africa, I asked my wife if she'd like a designer dress or diamonds as a present, but she said, "No, I want a divorce." I said I wasn't planning on spending that much.

—NICK FALDO

It hit a spectator, but my ball is OK.

—JERRY PATE

What did one golfer say to the other golfer?
Read any good greens lately?

—CHARLES SCHULZ

Putts get real difficult the day they hand out
the money.

—LEE TRAVINO

You know what they say about big hitters...the
woods are full of them.

—JIMMY DUMARET

An interesting thing about golf is that no matter how badly you play; it is always possible to get worse.

—BERYL DERANGED

I always feel that the hole is too small.

—MARK JAMES

One golfer a year is hit by lightning. This may be the only evidence we have of God's existence.

—STEVE AYLETT

You can make a lot of money out of golf. Just ask my ex-wives.

—LEE TREVINO

When I tee the ball where I can see it, I can't hit it. And when I put it where I can hit it, I can't see it.

—JACKIE GLEASON

Old golfers never die, they simply lose their drive.

—PETER DARBO

Why did the golfer wear an extra pair of trousers?
In case he got a hole in one.

—BERYL DERANGED

How many more bathroom-window curtains
must die needlessly to clothe golfers?

—MIKE LOUGH

My golf game and my butcher have one thing
in common: they both have a slice that's cost me
a fortune.

—ROBERT ORBEN

I'm not saying my golf game went bad, but if I grew tomatoes they'd come up sliced.

—LEE TREVINO

Although golf was originally restricted to wealthy, overweight Protestants, today it's open to anybody who owns hideous clothing.

—DAVE BARRY

The reason most people play golf is to wear clothes they would not be caught dead in otherwise.

—ROGER SIMON

"Play it as it lies" is one of the fundamental dictates of golf. The other is "Wear it if it clashes".

—HENRY BEARD

My neighbor was crying because her husband had left her for the tenth time. I consoled her, "Don't be unhappy, he'll be back." "Not this time," she sobbed. "He took his golf clubs."

—JOEY ADAMS

Daddy, why mustn't the ball go into the little hole?

—HERBERT V. PROCHNOW

My golf game's gone off so much that when I went fishing a couple of weeks ago my first cast missed the lake.

—BEN CRENSHAW

A handicapped golfer is anybody who plays with his boss.

—MILTON BERLE

Many a golfer yells "Fore", takes six and puts down five.

—HAROLD COFFIN

I don't rent a golf cart. I don't need one. Where I hit the ball, I can use public transportation.

—GENE PERRET

He quit playing golf, then took it up again 14 years later. He found his ball.

—BOB KALIBAN

More lampshades were broken in Britain by golf clubs than by Hitler's bombers.

—VAL DOONICAN

I own the erasers for all the miniature golf pencils.

—STEVEN WRIGHT

Golf: "I've had a good day when I don't fall out of the cart."

—BUDDY HACKETT

I'm into golf now. I'm getting pretty good. I can almost hit the ball as far as I can throw the clubs.

—BOB ETTINGER

Some of these legends have been around golf a long time. When they mention a good grip, they're talking about their dentures.

—BOB HOPE

My golf is improving. Yesterday I hit the ball in one!

—JANE SWAN

He's easy to spot on the golf course, his golf bag is white with a red cross on it.

—PETER DARBO

For me, the worst part of playing golf has always been hitting the ball.

—DAVE BARRY

My uncle has a different name for golf—connect the sand traps.

—GENE PERRET

On a recent survey, 80 percent of golfers admitted cheating. The other 20 percent lied.

—BRUCE LANSKY

But I really knew he was a golfer when he took three lumps of sugar and wrote down two.

—PETER DARBO

There are two types of doctor—the specialist who has trained his patients to become ill only during office hours and the general practitioner who may be called off the golf course at any time.

—AMBROSE BIERCE

I went golfing the other day, I dug up so many worms, I decided to go fishing!

—TOMMY COOPER

I'm not feeling too well. I need a doctor immediately. Quick, call the nearest golf course.

—GROUCHO MARX

The fairway is a narrow strip of mown grass that separates two groups of golfers looking for lost balls in the rough.

—HENRY BEARD

He's so old that when he plays golf, he doesn't have to yell "Fore". His bones creaking warns the foursome ahead of him.

—GENE PERRET

I swim a lot. It's either that or buy a new golf ball.

—BOB HOPE

What you must shoot to win a tournament?
The rest of the field.

—ROGER MALTBIE

"You know what your main trouble is?"
"What?"
"You stand too close to the ball after you've hit it."

—ERIC MORECAMBE
AND ERNIE WISE

"What's your excuse for coming home at this time of the night?"

"Golfing with friends, my dear."

"What? At 2 AM?!"

"Yes, We used night clubs."

—CURLY DAVID

Old golfers don't die.
They just putter out.

—SIL FOX

"Why do golfers wear two pairs of socks?"

"In case they get a hole in one."

—ANONYMOUS

"My wife says if I don't give up golf, she'll leave me."

"That's terrible."

"I know—I'm really going to miss her."

—ERIC MORECAMBE AND
ERNIE WISE

"Why aren't you playing golf with the colonel anymore?"

"What! Would you play with a man who swears and curses with every shot, who cheats in the bunkers and who enters false scores on his cards?"

"Certainly not!"

"Well, neither will the colonel."

—FREDDIE OLIVER

"Now," said the golf professional, "suppose you just go through the motions without hitting the ball."

"But that's precisely the difficulty I'm trying to overcome," said his pupil.

—ERIC SUTCLIFFE

"I have this extraordinary golf ball. If it goes into the rough, it sends out a radio bleep. If it falls into the water, it rises to the surface, and it glows in the dark."

"Amazing. Where did you get it?"

"I found it."

—ANONYMOUS

I liked Bob Hope's answer when someone asked, "How's your golf game?" He would say, "If it was a boxing match they'd stop it."

—ANONYMOUS

Work is the thing that interferes with golf.

—FRANK DANE

Hole-in-One

Hole-in-one—a stroke of genius.

—ROBERT MYERS

I play golf. I've never had a hole in one, but I hit a guy with a ball once, which is much better.

—MITCH HEDBERG

A hole-in-one is an occurrence in which a ball is hit directly from the tee into the hole on a single shot by a golfer playing alone.

—ROY MCKIE

The secret of golf is to turn three shots into two.

—BOBBY JONES

I used to play golf with a guy who cheated so badly that he had a hole-in-one and wrote down zero on his scorecard.

—BOB BRUCE

Hitting a tree in west Texas is stranger than getting a hole in one.

—MANCIL DAVIS

You can tell a good putt by the noise it makes.

—BOBBY LOCKE

A hole-in-one is amazing when you think of the different universes this white mass of molecules has to pass through on its way to the hole.

—MAC O'GRADY

The most important shot in golf is the next one.

—BEN HOGAN

Last week I missed a spectacular hole-in-one by only five strokes.

—BOB HOPE

If you have a hole-in-one in a competition you are in the last group and the bar is packed when you come in.

—CHRIS PLUMRIDGE

I played golf the other day—got a hole in one—
the other sock was perfect.

—TOMMY COOPER

Your first hole-in-one is always achieved when
playing alone.

—CHRIS PLUMRIDGE

I don't let birdies and pars get in the way of
having a good time.

—ANGELO SPAGNOLA

Ninety-five per cent of putts which finish short don't go in.

—HUBERT GREEN

I've just had a hole-in-one at the sixteenth and I left the ball in the hole just to prove it.

—BOB HOPE

Would you like to know how to sink those putts? Just hit the ball a little closer to the hole.

—VALERIE HOGAN

A bunker shot is the only shot in golf when you don't have to hit the ball.

—SANDY PARR

When your shot has to carry over a water hazard, you can either hit one more club or two more balls.

—HENRY BEARD

I've hit two balls into the water. I've a good mind to jump in and make it four.

—SIMON HOBDAY

As in Golf, So in Life

Golf isn't a game, it's a choice that one makes with one's life.

—CHARLES ROSIN

Never concede the putt that beats you.

—HARRY VARDON

The more I practice golf, the luckier I get.

—GENE SARAZEN

If I was told that I had two minutes left to live, I'd find a golfer to talk to because it would seem like forever.

—JEREMY THOMAS

Winning is not always the barometer of getting better.

—TIGER WOODS

All my life, as a golfer, I have tried to lay them cold and stiff at the holeside, and as a surgeon I have always tried to do the opposite.

—BERKELEY MOYNIHAN

The mind messes up more shots than the body.

—TOMMY BOLT

They say golf is like life, but don't believe them. Golf is more complicated than that.

—GARDNER DICKINSON

I never learned anything from a match that I won.

—BOBBY JONES

Golf without bunkers and hazards would be tame and monotonous.
So would life.

—B.C. FORBES

Golf is life. If you can't take golf, you can't take life.

—PETER DARBO

You learn very little about golf from life, but you learn a lot about life from golf.

—EARL WOODS

Forget your opponents, always play against par.

—SAM SNEAD

Golf is like life in a lot of ways. The most important competition is the one against yourself.

—BILL CLINTON

The real test of golf—and life—is not keeping out of the rough, but getting out after we are in.

—HENRY LASH

In golf, and in life, it's the follow through that makes the difference.

—PETER DARBO

Of all the hazards, fear is the worst.

—SAM SNEAD

Someone once told me that there is more to life than golf. I think it was my ex-wife.

—BRUCE LANSKY

You swing best when you have the fewest things to think about.

—BOBBY JONES

Hit it hard, go find it and hit it hard again.

—ARNOLD PALMER

That's life. The older you get, the tougher it is to score.

—BOB HOPE

Most people work all their life to be able to retire and play golf. I've played golf all my life to retire and go to work.

—JACK NICKLAUS

Look, there are no shortcuts in golf, and there are no shortcuts in life.

—TIGER WOODS

Go play golf. Go to the golf course. Hit the ball.
Find the ball. Repeat until the ball is in the hole.
Have fun. The end.

—CHUCK HOGAN

You can always become better.

—TIGER WOODS

Conclusion

Golf remains a staple in the lives of many modern sportsmen and women, providing them with a hobby, a purpose, or an outlet. It is their love for this sport that has kept it relevant throughout the years and will continue to do so. Each birdie and bogey comes with cherished memories and the added benefit of physical and mental improvement.

We hope that this collection has given you a renewed passion for the game and new insight into the way it has affected millions of others.

Now, anyone have time for a few holes?